SEARCHING

AT GROUND ZERO

SEARCHING FOR GOD
AT GROUND ZERO

A MEMOIR

JAMES MARTIN, S.J.

SHEED & WARD

Lanham, Maryland
Chicago, Illinois

2002

Published by Sheed & Ward
an imprint of Rowman & Littlefield Publishers, Inc.
4720 Boston Way
Lanham, MD 20706

12 Hid s Copse Road
Cumnor Hill, Oxford OX2 9JJ, England

Distributed by National Book Network

Printed in the United States of America

Cover design: Kathy Kikkert
Interior design: GrafixStudio, Inc.
Cover photography by Graham Morrison/AP
Author photo: Copyright Koby-Antupit, Cambridge, MA

Library of Congress Cataloging-in-Publication Data

Martin, James, S.J.
    Searching for God at ground zero / James Martin.
        p. cm.
    ISBN 1-58051-126-0 (pbk.)
        1. Martin, James, S.J.—Diaries. 2. Jesuits—New York
        (State)—New York—Diaries. 3. September 11
        Terrorist Attacks, 2001—Personal narratives. I. Title.

BX4705 .M412325 A3 2002
271'.5302—dc21
                                              2002066892
1 2 3 4 5 / 05 04 03 02

To the firefighters,
police officers,
and rescue workers
who gave their lives
in service to others
at the World Trade Center
on September 11, 2001.

INTRODUCTION

This is a journal of my time working among the rescue workers in the ruins of the World Trade Center in the days immediately following the terrorist attacks on September 11, 2001. By way of background, I am a recently ordained Catholic priest, age forty, and a member of a religious order called the Society of Jesus, more commonly known as the Jesuits. My job at the time was as an editor of a Catholic magazine based in New York City. But for the period described in this book, I felt drawn to set aside those responsibilities for a greater and more urgent need.

The days recounted in these pages were those I spent at the site. The days in between—the time spent working at the magazine—I deemed less relevant to the story. Likewise, I have not provided an account of the events of September 11, as this has already been done in other places, and with far greater accuracy than I could have accomplished.

Also, though the focus of this journal is the story of the firefighters, police officers, and rescue workers, I have not named any of the persons with whom I spoke, in order to afford them the privacy they deserve and, I think, have the right to expect.

Finally, my primary experience of working at the World Trade Center was that of a profound encounter with the presence of God. By saying this, I do not mean to deny that the site is also a place of unmitigated evil and intense sorrow. It is, of course, a grave. But having worked at the site meant that I was able to experience not only the sorrow that every American felt but also the hope that came from seeing how God revealed himself among the people laboring at "Ground Zero." In effect, I was a privileged witness to what many were perhaps not able to see: signs of God's presence in a place of great suffering.

And this is the story I hope to tell.

Thursday, September 13

Two days after the terrorist attack on the World Trade Center, I make my way to one of the emergency trauma centers in Manhattan. It has been hastily set up in a cavernous sports facility, called Chelsea Piers, on the Hudson River.

I had been to Chelsea Piers earlier, on the evening of September 11. Still stunned from the day's events, I wanted desperately, like many New Yorkers, to do something. But on that surreal and awful Tuesday night, I simply waited with dozens of doctors, nurses, police officers, firefighters, and volunteers for what we expected would be hundreds of survivors. At the trauma center, I ran into three Franciscan friars in long gray habits, full of energy and devotion, who were planning to spend the night. But though we wanted to help, after a few hours the stunning reality dawned: there would be few survivors to attend to.

When I return to Chelsea Piers two days later to offer assistance again, I discover that I have already been preceded by scores of clergy. "Another priest," says one harried, sweating volunteer as I enter. "Go upstairs and ask for Ellen."

I climb a flight of stairs and pass through a whitewashed cinder-block hallway. In a small room crowded with a dozen volunteers, Ellen sighs and tells me that she already has plenty of priests, ministers, and rabbis on hand.

I wander downstairs, trying to think about where I might be able to help most. Yesterday, I had volunteered at a counseling center set up by a local Catholic hospital, where family members painfully searched dog-eared sheets of paper for the names of survivors. But at the hospital too there was a surfeit of help: there are so many mental-health care professionals in Manhattan. Outside, surrounded by ambulances, U.S. Army jeeps, police cars, fire engines, and dump trucks, I ask a police sergeant a question upon which I had reflected not at all. But it seems the right thing to ask: Do you think they might be able to use a priest down there?

He knows where I mean. And I am terrified he will say yes.

Of course, he says, yes. He waves his hand and instantly a police car materializes to bring me to the site of the former World Trade Center. One of my Jesuit friends used to say that sometimes if God wants you to do something, he removes all the roadblocks, and I feel this intensely as we sail downtown: I ask, he answers, we go.

Fear increases dramatically with every southerly block. With me in the back seat is a well-dressed psychiatrist with a smartly clipped gray beard. He works in Manhattan and is planning on counseling some of the rescue workers. "Have you dealt with trauma victims?" he asks, as we speed through the city streets. No, I say, please give me some advice, and he does. "Just listen," he says. "That's the first thing."

The sights of the first part of the trip are familiar, comforting: on the right, the Hudson River, sparkling in the sunlight; on the left, the variegated Manhattan skyline. We make a left turn, and I notice fewer and fewer people walking on the streets. When we stop at an intersection, crowds of people surround our car, cheering, clapping, and waving tiny American flags. My window is open, and a hand is suddenly thrust in, offering me muffins, donuts, bottled water. "Thank you! Thank you!" they shout.

We turn again, and presently there are cars and taxicabs covered with a fine gray soot. Our car is waved through roadblocks manned by Army M.P.s. Photographers snap pictures of the car as we speed past, our sirens blaring.

We make a right turn: here are cars that have been crushed by falling debris, reams of papers floating in the breeze, and more and more pale gray soot coating the empty streets. We make another turn and I momentarily catch sight of a horribly twisted building. The psychiatrist gets out of the car, wishes me well, and sprints away.

The car turns once again, and I see the sight familiar to me from repeated viewings on television: the terrible remains of the World Trade Center, issuing forth a brown, acrid smoke that chokes one and brings tears to the eyes. It is repellent. I feel the urge at once to vomit and to weep.

The office buildings surrounding the site are in various states of destruction, collapse, and ruin. One building, perhaps twenty stories tall, looks as if a giant hand has simply clawed away its side; girders peel away from its facade. Windows are blown out in tall buildings for blocks around, and shards of glass litter the streets. Nearly thirty stories above us, a huge piece of one of the Trade Center towers has been impaled into the side of the American Express building. Everything I see frightens me with its scale and its violence.

The charred metal remains of the twin towers stand straight up from a pile of rubble and reach into the smoky sky. Because of the vast area of the destruction, it is somehow difficult to get a sense of the scale of the wreckage, and seeing the collapsed buildings is disorienting and confusing. I think, for some reason, of the tracery of ruined cathedrals in Europe: of Coventry in England, after the German bombings in the Second World War.

At the site are huge, milling crowds of people, almost all in uniform: firefighters in heavy black jackets with broad yellow stripes, police officers in navy suits, Army personnel in green-and-brown camouflage, and officials from every conceivable government agency wearing blue windbreakers emblazoned with their employer's name in yellow block letters: FEMA, OEM, OSHA, FBI. It is difficult to take everything in: the police cruisers with their screaming sirens; the Army M.P.s huddled together, gesticulating; the gas-masked police officers running across the plaza; the firefighters pouring oceans of water on the smoldering pile that was the Trade Center; the foul smoke; the shocking debris; the towering remains of the buildings.

And the realization that nearly three thousand people have been killed only two days before in the worst terrorist attack on American soil. It is one of the largest losses of American life in a single day, exceeded only by the number of those who died at the Battle of Antietam or on the beaches of Normandy on D-Day. More died here than at Pearl Harbor. I am before an immense tomb.

A U.S. Army soldier walks over to the car and greets me, providing me with a sort of friendly escort. Ashamed that I cannot tear my gaze from the site of the embrowned buildings, I make an effort to ask after the soldier's welfare. But, instead, he ministers to me.

"That's okay, Father," he says. "Everybody stares when they see it. It's hard to see it, isn't it?" He hands me a small white face mask, which I notice everyone is wearing, to protect against the noxious smoke and clouds of dust kicked up by each passing vehicle.

"Okay, Father," he says and points. "Just over there, that's where everyone is: it's the morgue." The temporary morgue is located inside a formerly tony office building—part of the World Financial Center—and one which, though I know the area well, I am totally unable to recognize.

The streets surrounding the morgue are covered with a half-inch of soot. More paper blows around; I notice an office memo, wet, its curled edges charred brown. It is a law office expense account. Twisted girders covered with grime must be stepped over.

All I can think of is a banality. But, though banal, it is true: this is like hell. Full of immense sadness and terror and pathos.

And yet, here is grace. Everyone assembled at this place is dedicated to the work of rescue; everyone is here for the other. All are purposeful, efficient, and hardworking.

Some of the firefighters and police officers sit by a "staging area," near the entrance of the temporary morgue, resting. Though most are New Yorkers, a surprising number are not, having traveled great distances (from Massachusetts, says one; from Indiana, says another) to help. We talk about what they have seen, how they feel, what they think. In the midst of this hell, they are inspiring to speak with, and say simple things, made profound to me by their situation: "Just doing my job, Father." "One day at a time." "Doing the best I can, Father." But I cannot resist the need to tell them what a wonderful job they are doing.

Suddenly I realize that I am standing beside grace. Here are men and women, some of whom tell me "I lost a buddy in there," who are going about their business. "Greater love has no person," said Jesus, "than the one who lays down his life for other." And this is what that looks like. Here it is. Living examples of what Jesus was talking about.

As I think this, three men carry a small, orange, vinyl bag past me, containing remains of a victim of the attack. I am afraid of what I will see so I do not look.

Three police officers sit in front of a pile of cardboard boxes, stacked perhaps six feet high. We talk about their work here. New Yorkers all, they say how strange it is to consider downtown without the twin towers. Many times they simply stare at the wreckage and shake their heads. We talk about friends we know who were near the Trade Center at the time.

One of my friends, I tell them, who worked at a nearby building, emerged from his subway station at 9 a.m. on Tuesday, as dozens of people raced by him. "What happened?" he asks someone. "A plane hit the World Trade Center!" He goes to his office anyway; he thinks that it is a small plane that must have hit. No need to worry. Once at his desk, he looks out the window and sees the appalling sight of the towers wreathed in smoke. When he tells me the story, he pauses and says what many New Yorkers say, "I couldn't believe it. I couldn't understand it." He then rushes to the stairwells with co-workers, and begins to race down eighteen floors. Once outside, a police officer shouts at him. "Run! Run! Run!" As my friend runs, dazed, someone yells at him, "It's collapsing!" He tells me later he thinks to himself: Don't be surprised if you die now.

Another close friend, a young Jesuit priest, is on his way to the school in New Jersey where he teaches. His subway train is halted at 9:00 that morning at the World Trade Center station. The first plane has already crashed into the north tower, and he emerges from the subway station into chaos. My friend runs toward the building to see if he can be of any help. As he draws nearer, a police officer shouts at him. "Get out of here!" From the towers, people flee in panic, and my friend finally begins to run with them. "I ran to Canal Street," he says, where he is told that one of the buildings has collapsed. When my friend tells me this, I think of how close he came to dying and how he does not mention this.

The police officers nod. They know many similar stories and, of course, far worse ones. It is hard to take it all in, they say. They talk about friends and partners who died in the collapse, and about their experiences over the last two days. They are worried that things will get even worse when the recovery of the bodies begins. "Here are the body bags," says one officer. He gestures behind him, and it is suddenly clear what is in that tall pile of boxes.

When I feel that I have talked with as many people as I can (at least those who are not busy with their work) I leave. One police sergeant tells me the way out: walk up this path. As I do, I pass streams of fire companies, and almost everyone greets me. There must be hundreds of firefighters. "Hello, Father," they say and touch the brims of their helmets. They shake my hand as I leave, and they move in toward the wreckage.

Leaving is stranger than arriving. And simpler: all I do is walk north. The rubble eventually recedes so there is nothing to step over; the soot becomes less distinct; the smoke clears and I remove my mask; there are more and more pedestrians. And suddenly I am back in New York on a sunny day: people in Greenwich Village sit idly in outdoor cafes, women in tank tops jog past, taxis race by. I remember reading about soldiers in World War I who would fight in the trenches in France during the morning and then, granted a day's leave, would be in the theaters of London at night. Is this what it is like for the rescue workers?

A subway entrance presents itself. A policeman spies me and walks over. I suddenly realize I must look strange: in a Roman collar, sweating, covered in gray ash, a face mask dangling from my chin. "Which subway do you want?" I am astonished to find out that I am so disoriented that I cannot tell him, but can only say that I want to go uptown. I feel foolish—New Yorkers take pride in knowing where they're going.

"Were you down there?" he asks. I nod, and he escorts me downstairs, past the ticket counter, and motions for the subway attendant to open up the gate, to allow me in for a free ride, a last gesture of kindness and solidarity in a city overwhelmed by grief but united by an overwhelming charity.

Friday, September 14

It has now become difficult, even in a Roman collar, to gain access to the site surrounding the Trade Center, which the press now refers to as "Ground Zero."

It is a phrase I find hard to use. With a Hollywood sound to it—like the title of a bad movie—it feels offensive, and somehow disrespectful, to the people who lie here and to their families and friends. The television news programs have already whipped up slick graphics and flashy logos ("America Attacked!") and special "theme" music to accompany their round-the-clock coverage.

It seems a trivialization of the event. Why does a tragedy need a logo and theme music anyway? I notice that most of the workers, instead of referring to "Ground Zero," say "the pile" or "down there" or, more simply, "the site."

At Chelsea Piers this afternoon, I hitch a ride in a huge tractor-trailer with two friendly ironworkers from New Jersey. Because of President Bush's visit today, their truck ends up being parked two miles from the site. The driver, however, expresses no impatience. "Why get angry?" he says. "There are more important things to worry about."

I thank them, climb down from the rig, and continue on foot down the West Side Highway, which is still closed to traffic. I make my way past four checkpoints, where one has to explain in detail one's intentions and present photo identification. Even here, though, there is the opportunity for ministry. The police officers and Army personnel who man the barricades are dog-tired after three days of work, little or no sleep, and an inhuman level of stress. Moreover, many have lost close friends in the collapse of the World Trade Center buildings. Still, they echo what so many say: they feel they should be at the site helping out more. "Those guys down there . . . ," says one, and shakes his head.

When I arrive, President Bush is about to appear; fighter jets and Army helicopters patrol noisily overhead. Waiting to enter the area is a massive crowd of firefighters, ironworkers, police officers, search-and-rescue teams, engineers, doctors, welders, truck drivers, counselors. A fireman stands beside me wearing a dusty yellow fire jacket. He tells me he's from Broward County. "Isn't that in Florida?" I ask.

He nods, and says that his chief had hesitated in sending his company to New York City, since many of the surrounding counties had already done so.

"Then how were you able to come?" I ask.

"My guys and I borrowed the truck and took two weeks as vacation time. We drove up nonstop." I am amazed by his generosity, but already realize that it is commonplace here.

We wait for two hours before the president leaves. It is easy to meet people in the crowd. I speak with two chaplains from the Port Authority, the quasi-governmental organization that, among its myriad duties, had owned and managed the World Trade Center. One of the Port Authority's offices was in the towers, and they have lost dozens of police officers and civilians. One chaplain, named Father Mark, suggests that it might be easier for me to gain access to the site if I were an "official" chaplain, and he offers to arrange this for me through the Port Authority.

Standing beside Father Mark is a psychologist named Lynn, from a nearby college, who is helping with the Red Cross's efforts in grief counseling. I am amazed by the work of the Red Cross here: they are well organized, professional, and omnipresent.

Lynn offers some useful and sensible tips on how best to counsel the rescue workers. "Just let them talk," she says. "If they become hysterical, get them to focus on the everyday things in their life. Ask them what they had for breakfast, where they're from, and how long it's been since they've slept." I am grateful for her advice.

Clouds form overhead and the air turns chilly. I mention to Lynn that I was foolish for not having brought a heavier jacket. She suggests I visit the Salvation Army van and ask for a coat. I tell her that I don't want to take a coat from someone who might need it more—a tired rescue worker or a cold firefighter. "Are you kidding?" she says. "They have hundreds of them. Just go and ask."

As I wander over to the Salvation Army station, a heavy man wearing glasses sprints over to me. "Father," he says, "will you bless my truck? It's brand new." He points to a long white van that reads "SPCA." My initial reaction is one of ignorant indignation: Is this really the time to be thinking about pets?

But the van, it turns out, is for the search-and-rescue dogs. Dogs have been brought here by police departments from across the country to assist in the rescue efforts. Sadly, the dogs, who are trained to locate living human beings, have been unable to do so: there are simply not enough live victims. As a result, the dogs have grown increasingly depressed and anxious. The SPCA man explains that to keep the animals alert, firefighters have volunteered to lie inert on the rubble and "allow" the dogs to discover them.

The van, I see, is a place for the rescue dogs to rest and to be fed and watered. A woman massages a tired golden retriever hooked up to an I.V. drip. When I see the efforts of those who work with the dogs, I am ashamed by my initial reaction. With the SPCA man beside me, I say a prayer asking God to bless the van, and I ask the intercession of St. Francis of Assisi, the patron saint of animals, for good measure.

Just then an enormous rig pulls up, carrying John Deere "Gators"—small, green, six-wheel jeeps—on its flatbed trailer, which I assume will be used for the transport of workers around the site. The truck rumbles to a halt and a man climbs down from the cab. "Father," he says, "will you bless my rig?" He wears a crucifix around his neck. As I begin to pray an improvised blessing, he bows his head and crosses himself.

The friendly, gray-haired, grandmotherly woman at the Salvation Army van offers me a green fleece zip-up jacket. On the left breast pocket is an embroidered picture of a cow above the words "Monroe Dairy: East Providence, R.I." I pull it on and am instantly warmed. I think of the people in Providence who donated the jacket, and say a prayer for them.

When I find my way back to Lynn, she is talking to a New York City policeman. She laughs when she sees the jacket. The policeman says, "Father, between your collar and that cow jacket, people aren't going to know *who* you're representing!"

When the M.P.s finally open the cordon, the huge mass of humanity streams in, eager to begin their work. As I walk in I meet another fireman, who stops to talk. He is a tall, big man, covered in ash, who extends a cut and bloodied hand to shake. "Hello, Padre." We talk about his work over the past few days. Again, like many of the rescue workers, if he is not working directly on the "bucket brigade," he feels as if he is not doing enough. But today he has been allowed to work there. And suddenly he begins to weep. "This morning they pulled out a baby," he says. Taking a cue from Lynn, I ask the man to talk about what he is feeling and what he saw. In a few moments his tears stop. He thanks me, shakes my hand, and continues toward the site.

I am overwhelmed by what I can only describe as an experience of the presence of God's Spirit: an almost tangible sense of charity and generosity. First, of course, there is the shared awareness that we are working at a place where hundreds of firefighters and dozens of police officers sacrificed their lives for others. This silent witness informs every act and word. There is also the living witness of those who continue this work in the midst of their mourning: firefighters who have lost their "brothers," NYPD officers who have lost their partners, Port Authority police who have lost their friends. And there is the presence of volunteers who manifest extraordinary generosity: some have driven hundreds of miles to be here and, after their arrival, they sleep little or not at all. They freely donate their time, their energy, their selves.

But the presence of the Holy Spirit is felt in another, more powerful way. It is in the profound sense of community that one encounters once inside the perimeter of the site. And today I realize what it is that I have been noticing since yesterday: everyone is kind. I have not met one person who is not friendly, solicitous, and generous. The police officers and soldiers are patient and polite at the barricaded checkpoints. On the way into the site, Salvation Army volunteers cheerfully offer me sodas, bottled water, and candy bars. The firefighters who work during their grief and shock ask how I am doing. And one is surrounded by the physical signs of charity as well: food, clothing, tents, trucks, blankets and, most touching of all, hundreds of handwritten notes from elementary-school children.

Here it feels as if everyone is working together for a common good. It is an experience of love and community unlike any I have ever known. And to me it signals the presence of the Holy Spirit. For it is the Spirit that brings unity and concord, that causes peace and harmony, that banishes division and strife.

Tonight at dinner in my community I will mention this to my brother Jesuits. I cannot get it out of my mind. As a Jesuit, I have worked in a variety of settings—in hospitals, schools, homeless shelters, parishes, and retreat houses; among street-gang members in Chicago; with refugees in East Africa; alongside the poor in the slums of Kingston, Jamaica. But I have never experienced the Spirit as powerfully as I have at Ground Zero.

Someone mentions how different that is from the behavior of the terrorists. One Jesuit says he had read that one of the last things some of the terrorists did was to argue. On the night before their awful flights, as they drank in a local bar, they argued. During the flight they argued with one another. Their last days, it seems, were ones of dissent and discord.

Suddenly, at the dinner table, it makes sense to me. God's Spirit—as Jesus and St. Paul and all the saints have said—leads to unity, harmony, and peace. Turning away from the Spirit leads to tension, violence, and hatred.

It is a strikingly clear example of how the Spirit works, almost like a lesson. And it is so easy to see at the World Trade Center.

But is it, in the end, so surprising that in a place of such evil and such horror, in a place where so many have suffered and died, that God would pour out his Spirit in such a new and powerful way?

SATURDAY, SEPTEMBER 15

This morning a fellow Jesuit named Bob and I plan on going to the Trade Center together. I'm grateful for the company: Bob's a close friend, and it's good to be here with another Jesuit priest. As we approach the first checkpoint, we see a phalanx of police officers, and wonder if we will be allowed in. We say a prayer, asking the intercession of Pedro Arrupe to help us get into the site.

Father Arrupe, the former superior of the Jesuit Order, was working as the director of novices in Hiroshima, Japan, in 1945. When the atomic bomb was dropped on his city, Arrupe, who had studied medicine before entering the Jesuits, rushed to the site to care for the wounded. He quickly turned the Jesuit novitiate into a makeshift hospital and witnessed what he called "the working of charity in people."

Perhaps thanks to the intercession of Father Arrupe—or perhaps thanks to the policeman who graduated from a Jesuit college—we pass easily.

Once inside, we slowly make our way around, talking to rescue workers. They are still facing a welter of emotions: disorientation, sadness, anger, confusion, and frustration. Nearly everyone is exhausted.

After an hour, Bob and I stumble upon the World Trade Center's Catholic chapel, which I hadn't even known existed. On the first floor of an apartment building a few hundred yards from the Trade Center, tiny St. Joseph's chapel appears as a simple, storefront church. Today, though, it has been commandeered to serve as a sort of supply depot: the dimly lit space is filled with boxes of shoes, socks, hard hats, underwear, gas masks, flashlights.

The man running the supply depot is named Flick, a cheerful, efficient New Yorker with long black hair and a closely cropped beard. Flick tells us that he began working here on the night of September 11. That night, he simply showed up, hoping to pitch in, and began unloading boxes of supplies at the dock. Flick proved such a good organizer that the police awarded him official credentials and he became, *de facto*, in charge of supplies for the rescue workers. He has slept here every night since the attack.

By virtue of his position, Flick also seems to be in charge of the chapel itself, so we ask him: Would it be okay if we celebrated Mass for the rescue workers tomorrow, outside?

Sure, he says.

We tell Flick that we hope to celebrate Mass at 9 a.m. and at 2 p.m.

But a young man standing next to us interrupts our conversation. "Excuse me, Father," he says. On his fleece zip-up jacket he wears two large pieces of masking tape. One with his name and one that reads "Chaplain."

"I think it's best that there be no proselytizing here," he says.

I assume that he's overheard our conversation with Flick, so I explain. "Well, it's an outdoor Mass," I say. "We're certainly not going to force anyone to come, and besides, most of these guys are Catholics."

He frowns and shakes his head in protest.

"You know, Father," he says testily. "What these men really need is for you to go out and talk to them, not to spend all of your time in the chapel."

Having spent the last two days doing exactly that, I am insulted and annoyed, but decide it more prudent not to argue. It strikes me that in my short time here, the first dispute I encounter is a religious one, and this embarrasses me. In any event, the last thing people need here is arguments, so I fall silent. He turns away and begins correcting someone for having placed a box of socks in the wrong place.

Flick turns to me. "So what time did you want to say that Mass?"

"Don't I have to clear it with him?" I say, pointing to the disapproving chaplain.

Flick leans close. "Father," he says, whispering, "let me tell you something. I don't know who the fuck he is. I don't know what he does or where he's from. So you have Mass whenever you want."

I tell him we'll celebrate at 9 a.m. and 2 p.m.

While we are talking near the altar, someone asks us to be quiet and points. Behind the altar, where a priest would stand during Mass, two firemen are curled in sleep next to each other, fully clothed, covered in grime.

Outside the chapel, Bob turns to me. "Hooray for Flick," he says.

• • •

What I fear the most is helping with the dead bodies or the body parts that the rescue workers are recovering. A fire department chaplain we meet says that much of his work consists of praying over the bodies, for the consolation of those gathered. But I wonder if I will be able to do even this. My friend Bob, though, has less fear than I do, and convinces me that we should visit the morgue.

Outside the temporary morgue is a large white tent, set up beside the Merrill Lynch building at the World Financial Center. Stepping under the tent is almost like entering a chapel. An Episcopal priest prays quietly, and the police officers are utterly silent as they stare at the full black body bag that lies on the ground. Bob and I join in the prayer, and I wonder who lies in the bag, who grieves for this person, who waits for news of this person. I want to tell the families and friends of the victims what a holy place they have made this tent into.

Around noon we find ourselves hungry. And, thanks to nationwide generosity, food is plentiful at the site. Seven-foot-high piles of Poland Spring water jugs are stacked behind the World Financial Center. A few hundred feet from Ground Zero, near the chapel, a Salvation Army stand offers all manner of snacks: candy bars, Rice Krispie bars, granola bars, cookies, Gatorade, bottled water, fruit juices, and soda. Near Chambers Street are parked four large food trucks, including a McDonald's van, where an efficient but busy staff serves burgers, French fries, sodas, and milk shakes to hungry workers.

Next to the temporary McDonald's is still another Salvation Army stand that today offers, among other things, Styrofoam cups of steaming split-pea soup, bottles of neon-colored energy drinks, and paper plates piled high with spaghetti and meatballs.

For the last two days, though, many of the rescue workers have been encouraging me to eat on "the boat." Docked at the marina before the attacks were an assortment of small boats used largely for corporate parties. These boats enjoyed a thriving business of ferrying passengers around New York harbor for daytime and evening cruises. Now a large white, three-story cruise boat has been donated to the relief effort to serve as a dining facility. Though it is certainly the best place for a hot meal and a chance to relax, I have avoided it: I was loath to use something that had been set up for the workers. But now, with Bob and I planning to put in a full day's work, we feel like we are part of the team, and decide to try it out.

The line of workers waiting to board the boat snakes around the dock. They stand patiently in the bright sunlight, talking in small groups of like professions: firefighters, welders, soldiers, steelworkers, counselors, Salvation Army volunteers, sanitation workers. After a half-hour's wait, we climb aboard the rickety metal staircase and are directed into the main dining area. Decorating the walls of the dining room are brightly colored construction-paper posters made by American schoolchildren. In red, white, and blue, with drawings of flags, eagles, the Liberty Bell, George Washington, and the World Trade Center, they are similar to others that are posted everywhere around the site. My favorite is from a third-grade schoolgirl to the "firefiters" that reads: "I am sure whatever you are doing right now you are helping someone."

The main dining room, warm and redolent of the smell of lasagna, roast chicken, and coffee, is crammed with hundreds of workers clustered around dozens of round wooden tables. Firemen eat with FEMA officials, police officers hand water bottles to ironworkers, counselors break bread with search-and-rescue teams, soldiers clear room at their table for a Red Cross counselor, truck drivers offer to fetch a cup of coffee for a state trooper.

It is a strangely beautiful sight, and I am surprised to be reminded of a phrase from my theology studies. Here, I think, is a powerful image of the Kingdom of God. It's odd to think of something like this in a place of such suffering and misery, but the image is unavoidable for me. Here is everyone eating together, working together, talking with one another, sharing stories, encouraging one another, united in the common work of charity. It's difficult not to think of it as a sort of eucharistic meal— a breaking of bread in the spirit of sacrifice and remembrance. At the very least, the room seems suffused with the presence of God.

Bob and I sit down with an elderly policeman with a deeply lined face and graying hair, who talks about his work. He has been retired for five years, but has returned to offer his services today. "Look up that way," he says pointing north, where brilliant sunshine glitters on the Hudson River and illuminates the World Financial Center's tall buildings. "It's beautiful, isn't it?"

"Now look over there," he says, and points behind him, in the direction of the still-smoldering rubble pile. "It's hard to believe it's the same world, huh?"

As it turns out, he is a deeply religious Southern Baptist, who wants to talk about good and evil. God, says the retired policeman, would not want any of this destruction, but God has brought everyone together here. He pauses.

"It's the work of the Spirit," he says.

After a few minutes, we finish our meal and say goodbye to the police officer. "God bless you!" he calls out as we walk across the dining room.

Bob and I clank down the metal stairs and, as we move into the plaza, I catch sight of the name of the cruise line emblazoned on the side of the boat. The huge black letters read: "Spirit Cruise."

• • •

The rest of our afternoon is spent circulating among the workers, listening, listening, listening. There is still a near-universal sense of shock and disorientation. The firefighters and police officers are still entirely focused on retrieving any of their "buddies" who may yet be alive under the rubble. Most still stare at the site, as if expecting it to yield answers. They shake their heads and express their disbelief. Surprisingly few seem angry, but perhaps they are simply too tired for this: anger takes energy. Sometimes Bob and I pray with the workers. And today I have started to ask who they knew in the twin towers, so we can pray for their friends by name. When I say their friends' names aloud, some weep.

Before we leave, Bob and I pause in front of the wreckage of the World Trade Center, a few yards from where they pulled out the body we saw earlier in the morgue. Behind us looms the latticed remains of the tower walls, as well as the monstrous rubble pile: mangled girders, broken glass, pulverized concrete, rising six or seven stories—it's difficult to tell, so disorienting are the surroundings. It is a malevolent site: a symbol of evil. But it is also a sacred site: a tomb of innocents.

Bob and I say a prayer for the victims, and I think of the thousands who lie here: people we do not know, but each of whom is known intimately by God.

Sunday, September 16

Today I have returned with Bob and a group of Jesuit seminarians, three of whom are studying at Fordham University in the Bronx—Andrew, Joe, and Phillip—as well as Pawel, a Polish seminarian working at a nearby Jesuit middle school. We meet at 7:30 a.m. in Pawel's community, and, before leaving, we pray for the work of the day.

We make our way on foot to one of the checkpoints, but discover an immense crowd of workers waiting to enter. Our own entrance now looks unlikely, and we worry about the surfeit of Army M.P.s, who may not be as accommodating as the Irish American police officers who greeted us in the past. As it turns out, officials are sweeping the area this morning as a "crime scene," and Ground Zero is effectively shut down. The military police instruct us to wait in the long line of workers hoping to enter the site. Our collars, then, prove largely ineffective in securing entrance. (Bob reminds me that we had forgotten to pray to Pedro Arrupe.)

Two hours pass, and Bob and Joe are forced to leave for other appointments. I am disappointed they will not be allowed in. I also wonder if anyone is waiting for the 9 a.m. Mass.

Eventually, a police officer named Kelly says we can enter. "What about the M.P.s?" I ask. "Don't worry, Father," he says, and waves us in.

Once inside, Andrew, Phillip, Pawel, and I move around, meeting rescue workers as we go. When we finally reach Ground Zero, we see a group of family members of the police officers lost in the collapse of the towers. As they leave in a jeep, one shouts back at the site, "We love you!"

At 11:00, we set up for Mass a few yards away. In the dusty plaza we discover a cast-off table, which we cover with a white sheet we have brought with us. Borrowed chalices and patens from a nearby Jesuit chapel are placed on the table next to a Poland Spring water bottle, a hard hat, and a respirator. But before we can begin, a firefighter warns us that an electric transformer has been found in the rubble and will be exploded, which may release carcinogenic P.C.B.s into the air. It is best for us to avoid the area, he says. I worry that I have placed the

Jesuit seminarians in some sort of danger. We duck back into the chapel, and when it seems that there, in fact, will be no explosion, we again assemble outside with our respirators. In a few minutes a small group of people gather around the table: all visibly tired, all covered with sweat, all blanketed in ash.

We move through the Mass quickly: these are busy people. When it comes time for the Gospel, I find it difficult to read aloud—it is almost painfully appropriate. It is about the God who searches for and rescues us.

In the fifteenth chapter of the Gospel of Luke, Jesus offers two short parables designed, like every parable, to invite the listener to think about what God is like. God, says Jesus, is like a shepherd. "Which one of you, having a hundred sheep and losing one of them, does not leave the ninety-nine in the wilderness and go after the one that is lost, until he has found it? When he has found it, he lays it on his shoulder and rejoices."

And, says Jesus, God is like a woman with ten silver coins.

"If she loses one of them, does she not light a lamp, sweep the house, and search carefully until she finds it?"

So around the altar we speak of the God who constantly searches for us, desires to rescue us, and rejoices when we are found. God desires nothing more than to help us find our way to him. And this is the God who accompanies us today, as we search and rescue—as we perform work that, in effect, mirrors God's own activity in the world.

After Mass we stand by the makeshift altar with the ciborium, as dust and rescue workers swirl around us. Many come for Communion. A burly police officer from the search-and-rescue team, wearing the cumbersome equipment of his trade—a heavy vest, oversized flashlight, plastic respirator, and high-tech tools—asks to receive the Eucharist. When I raise the host from the ciborium, he falls to his knees in the plaza, amidst the broken glass, burnt paper, and gray ash. Some ask for confession. And I think that these men, whatever their sins, have already done their penance.

Some ask for a blessing. Others ask for counsel. An African American policeman approaches Pawel and I overhear him ask for "a word of comfort." Though I wonder how a Polish Jesuit new to the U.S. will be able to communicate with the man, they speak for ten minutes.

After they finish speaking, Pawel comes to me and says quietly, "Have you seen the sign?" Around the site are large plywood boards that have been spray-painted with neon orange paint to indicate various functions. "Morgue," says one sign. "Eye-wash station," says one. "Broken glass," says another. I follow Pawel to the sign that someone, unknown to us, has leaned against chairs a few feet from our little altar. It reads: "Body of Christ."

It astonishes us. The anonymous sign-maker could just as easily have written "Mass" or "Eucharist" or even "Catholic services." Perhaps having heard us repeat "the Body of Christ" over and over as firefighters and police officers approached the altar, the sign-maker decided that this was what we were offering at this place. And he or she was right. But the plywood board, with its crude orange letters, points to something else. For me, the sign says: Here is the Body of Christ, broken and bloodied, lying amidst the destruction. Here is the Body of Christ, the community, working together in this place. Here is the Body of Christ, offering new life, awaiting resurrection. Here is the Body of Christ, holding out hope for all of you who work here, for all of you who lie here. Here is the Body of Christ—with you.

Phillip leaves after the Mass, and Andrew and Pawel and I decide to walk around the plaza and talk to as many people as we can.

At 2:00, a fireman, still wearing his heavy black-and-yellow fire jacket, runs up to Andrew and me. "Father," he says breathlessly, "are you still saying Mass at 2:00?"

I had forgotten that yesterday we had promised that we would do so. And I think: Here is devotion. An exhausted man working in an unimaginable setting, on his short break, decides he will go to Mass and, finding the priest not there, sets out to find him.

The next day the Gospel reading, again from Luke, will be of the Roman soldier who asks Jesus to heal his slave. When Jesus asks to come to his house, the soldier responds that there is no need for this. All Jesus needs to do is to say the word. I have men under my command, explains the soldier: "I say *Come here* and he comes, or *Do this* and he does it." Jesus responds, "Not even in Israel have I found such faith." When I read this story, I think of the firefighter who searches for Mass at the construction site. When have I seen such faith?

I think of everyone else here too, in this place of death, where the Holy Spirit is more present than anywhere I have ever been: here, at this site, where God has said to so many rescue workers, *Come here*, and they have come, *Do this*, and they are doing it.

• • •

Leaving the site, Andrew, Pawel, and I walk up the West Side Highway, which has been closed off to city traffic for the past three days. Standing on the other side of the barricades is a crowd of two or three hundred people who cheer as workers leave the site. Many wave flags and hold up handmade signs and posters with encouraging messages. In a window of one of the buildings facing the street someone has placed a stereo speaker. The voice of Kate Smith singing "God Bless America" echoes loudly up and down the West Side Highway, over the noise of the cheering crowd.

As each flatbed truck, tractor-trailer, police cruiser, Army vehicle, jeep, limousine, or fire truck passes the crowd, a boisterous cheer goes up.

"Thank you!"

"We love you!"

"You're my hero!"

I'm happy for the rescue workers: they deserve the praise and need the encouragement. And I'm happy for those in the crowd too: many in the city are desperate to help in any way they can, and this is a wonderful way to do so.

As we draw closer to the barricades, a fire truck crammed with firemen in blue T-shirts and overalls passes by, and the crowd roars its approval. "You're heroes! You're heroes!"

Near the final police checkpoint, a trio of college-age students hands us some bottled water and candy bars. "Thanks," says Andrew.

"No, no, no," says a lanky college-age boy with a silver ring through his eyebrow. "Thanks to you."

After the fire truck passes, we walk up the street, and I am surprised to hear the crowd burst into another cheer—though there are no trucks or cars or vans around.

"Who are they cheering for now?" says Pawel.

I laugh, it seems for the first time in days. "They're cheering for you!"

A phalanx of television news vans is stationed on the sidewalk a few feet from the barricades. The rescue work has attracted worldwide coverage, and hundreds of TV stations have quickly staked out their territory in the streets surrounding the perimeter. White plastic tents shelter the reporters and camera crews from the blazing sun. And with no direct access to the site, reporters are desperate to interview anyone who emerges from the area, and we present obvious "gets."

Andrew, Pawel, and I are immediately stopped and interviewed by, in rapid succession, a Paris-based daily newspaper, a local radio station, and, finally, a weekly newspaper in Niagara, New York. While the Niagara reporter peppers us with questions, a photographer takes our pictures.

"Okay," he says, "take off your gas mask. And take off your hard hat."

Idiotically, I do what he tells me as I answer the reporter's questions. The photographer snaps his camera. Then he says, "Okay. Look somber."

It's a horrible thing to say, insulting and callous. I instantly fill with anger, though I am too tired to say so. All I want to do now is go home.

On the whole, however, the press has succeeded in the important work of spreading stories of heroism, bravery, and charity. And it is these stories that have spurred the mass donations of food, water, and clothing, and have impelled hundreds of New Yorkers to line the West Side Highway and give voice to their support. Overall, the public has responded to these stories with astonishing generosity.

It is also clear that something in the public has responded, in particular, to the tales of the firefighters running into the burning buildings. Over and over, people express something akin to amazement at the image of firemen racing into the doomed towers, ready to lay down their lives, even as thousands flee. There is a photograph, widely circulated, taken by an office worker escaping from one of the towers, that shows just this: a fireman burdened with nearly a hundred pounds of gear, laboring up a stairwell, making his way past those desperate to escape, who look on, astonished. It is an arresting image that is widely commented upon. Indeed, it seems to shock people.

And it shocks people, I suspect, for two reasons.

First, it is what one might call a "countercultural" image. In general, ours is a culture in which the self is preeminent, in which fame is prized, and in which money is the ultimate (if not only) measure of success and worth. But the actions of the firefighters fly directly in the face of these values. The men who raced into the World Trade Center buildings were wholly unconcerned with self (indeed, totally other-directed), not seeking for fame (nor, on an individual basis, did they receive it), and willing to perform heroic deeds without the promise of financial reward. Their actions were profoundly countercultural. So they shocked us.

Second, the story of the firefighters, I think, speaks to the part of ourselves that recognizes the fundamentally religious image of the one who lays down his life for others. It is not difficult to draw a clear, bright line from the firefighters and police officers who race into a burning building in order to save others, to Jesus of Nazareth offering up his life out of love for the salvation of humankind.

This is not to say that the rescue workers who lost their lives in the terrorist attacks were saints or perfect or somehow divine. But that's the point: they were human beings who were showing us how God loves, how God is. Just as a parable shows us this. And something within us naturally responds to this image of the divine. Here, I think, is God revealing himself in a clear and powerful way during a time of intense sadness and widespread confusion.

A parable, the great Scripture scholar C. H. Dodd wrote, is "a metaphor or simile drawn from nature or common life, arresting the hearer by its vividness or strangeness, that leaves the mind in sufficient doubt about its precise application to tease it into active thought." For Jesus of Nazareth, God and the kingdom of God were altogether impossible to explain—except with stories. Theological explanations and philosophical definitions fall short: they cannot adequately contain the mystery of God and God's kingdom. Jesus grasped this, and so instead he offered his disciples parables. Jesus' stories of the woman and her lost coin and the shepherd searching for his sheep are both parables for his times: designed to teach his listeners about selflessness, about love, and about God.

The story of the rescue workers at the World Trade Center is a parable for our times: offered by God to teach us about selflessness, and about love. About who God is and how God is.

WEDNESDAY, SEPTEMBER 19

It's been two days since I last came to the World Trade Center. My Jesuit friends suggested—some gently, some not so gently—that I should take a few days off, and indeed, I had felt tremendously drained after the past three days at the site. But it's embarrassing to admit this, for I know how infinitely more tiring and draining it must be for the rescue workers.

One of the people with whom I've spoken recently is my friend George, a Jesuit who works as a prison chaplain in Boston. On the telephone late one night I confide to him that I feel guilty about not working down there around the clock.

What's more, I feel tremendously guilty that what I am seeing in lower Manhattan is beginning to seem familiar. I am horrified that I am beginning to feel—it is hard for me even to say this to George—almost at home there. Somehow it feels disrespectful to the ones who still lie beneath the rubble. But based on his own work in a difficult setting, George counsels that it's natural to lose one's initial feelings of horror and shock. Otherwise, he asks, how could you minister? "As long as you don't lose your feeling of compassion," he says. "That's what matters most." George also suggests I take some time off.

So on Monday I do not go to the site, and instead decide to spend the day at the magazine. (I have already fallen far behind in my editorial work.) But though I see the wisdom of my friends' advice—you're only human, everyone needs a break, you'll be more useful if you're rested, etc.—I am nonetheless overcome with guilt as I sit at my desk. I can't help wondering how things are going downtown. And I wonder how I can justify taking any time off right now, when so much needs to be done downtown. The firefighters get no break, I think. Why should I get one?

After a few hours of distracted work, I begin to wonder when I will be able to return. And, having read in the newspaper about tightened security, I also wonder if it will be even more difficult to gain access to the site. I remember that Father Mark, the chaplain I had met on Friday, had offered to arrange some credentials for me. Rummaging through my wallet, I fish out his business card and telephone number.

Over the phone, Father Mark is friendly and helpful, and offers to call the chief of the Port Authority Police Department. Would I be able to see him today? he asks.

My guilt finally gets the better of me: Sure, I say.

After ten minutes he calls back, having already arranged an appointment for me. And in a few hours I am on my way to the offices of the Port Authority, across the Hudson River in Jersey City, where I am officially deputized as a chaplain and given a gold metal badge and a blue windbreaker emblazoned with the Port Authority seal. I am grateful for this, as I know it will help me and the other Jesuits do our ministry more easily.

They issue me an identification card, too, which I find unaccountably moving. Though it is already one week after the tragedy, the legend below my photo reads: "Appointed 09/11/01."

The next day, I realize that the amount of work at the magazine has by now become too great to ignore, and I plow through a week's worth of reading manuscripts, editing articles, and reviewing galleys.

• • •

But this morning, I have returned with Andrew. It is a bright, crystalline day, as it has been on many of the past days: a perfect Indian summer morning. But the lovely weather seems incongruous, almost insulting, in the emotional shadow of the Trade Center.

What I had read in the papers is confirmed: security has become increasingly tighter, and many more uniformed guards are stationed at the checkpoints. As a result, Andrew and I first spend a good deal of time speaking with the men and women guarding the perimeter: National Guard personnel who have lately flown in from upstate New York and who are shocked by what they see; New York state troopers who say that they have an "easy" job compared with the men on the bucket brigade; and Army M.P.s who apologize profusely when they ask to see our identification, and who then talk about their feelings about working here. One soldier says that he spent two years in Vietnam, but never expected to see something like this in his own country. "Never in a million years," he says, and his eyes well with tears.

Once we pass the perimeter, we meet a fireman who confesses how overwhelmed he is from the long hours, the sadness, and the stress of the work of recovery and rescue. He finds it difficult to sleep at night and nearly impossible to relax. "When I go home," he explains, "all I want to do is turn on the TV and get my mind off of *that*." He gestures toward the pile. "But all they have on

TV is news about the work down here. It's like I can't escape it."

Still, he says, he feels that—despite his pain—he's not doing enough. This is a common theme, both here and around the city. Everyone feels they should be doing more. Sometimes, when friends say that what they are doing is insufficient, I will ask what they have done so far. And usually they have already acted with great generosity: giving blood, donating money, bringing food to their local firehouse. So I tell them that whatever they've done, it's bound to be helpful in some way, however small. What's more, the desire to help and the intention of charity are in themselves good things. In this life, I think, we do as much as we can and, in hope, leave the rest up to God.

I also tell my friends that, paradoxically, the same feelings are expressed at the site itself. And the closer you draw to the epicenter of the site, the greater and more poignant this paradox grows. I have come to think of this as concentric circles of humility. When we ask after the welfare of the National Guardsmen at the checkpoints, they shake their heads and say that, even though they are pulling down long hours, they are not the ones doing the tough work. "Those guys on the pile," they say, "they're the ones who have it rough."

And when at the site we speak to rescue workers who are taking a few days off from the bucket brigade, they say they too should be doing more: they should be back on the rubble pile. Finally, when you meet guys coming off their shifts from the pile—that is, precisely those people whom the rest of the world imagines as laboring at Ground Zero—even *they* resist the notion that they have done enough.

"We're not the heroes, Father," one of them tells me today. "The guys who gave their lives: they're the heroes."

• • •

Stopping by the little chapel near the World Financial Center, which is still being used as a supply depot, Andrew and I meet two gregarious Hispanic American volunteers, a married couple. They tell us that they have been working here for three days, even though the woman is pregnant. We begin to talk about their work but they suddenly switch the topic. They're worried about what the bishop told them. "What bishop?" says Andrew.

Yesterday, they explain, someone identifying himself as "a bishop from Rome" came to tour the site and wandered into the chapel. Admittedly, the chapel—now crowded with torn cardboard boxes overflowing with shoes, boots, and gloves; sloppy piles of blankets; cast-off hard hats; rumpled sleeping bags and hundreds of loose respirators and gas masks—is definitely in need of some sprucing up. On the wall near a statue of St. Joseph someone has written the word "Shoes" in blue magic marker. The chapel's cushioned chairs, filthy with dust and grime, are scattered outside on the plaza, where rescue workers relax on them when they eat.

But, given the circumstances, the chapel has held up remarkably well. And it seems to me that the chapel is being put to a wonderful use: providing much-needed supplies for the rescue workers and offering a quiet place in this noisy locale for firefighters and police officers to sleep. In ways that it probably never has before, the chapel is now performing the traditional "corporal works of mercy": feeding the hungry, giving drink to the thirsty, sheltering the homeless, and clothing the naked. It has become a place of comfort and relief, the sort of soul of the relief effort. Some Orthodox monks have even placed two small white candles on the marble altar as a sign of the chapel's continuing holiness.

"The bishop was really upset," continues the man. "It looked like he was gonna have a heart attack or something. He just kept saying how horrible it was and how we had desecrated it and how he would have to call Rome."

The man and woman, who say they only want to be good Catholics, look distraught. In response, we tell them that the little chapel is being put to good use: they have certainly done nothing wrong. I also tell them I seriously doubted the man was actually a bishop (what bishop would say such a thing anyway?) and, in any event, unless he was *the* Bishop of Rome, that is, the Pope, he had no authority. We pray a blessing for their work and for their baby before we leave.

Afterwards, Andrew and I decide to split up, as it has seemed easier to strike up conversations with people when we work alone. I make my way behind the World Financial Center, where dozens of rescue workers rest on the chairs that have been set up in the broad esplanade that fronts the Hudson River. One man looks particularly incongruous: instead of a uniform he wears a green windbreaker, a neat button-down shirt, and pressed trousers. Fifty-ish with thinning hair, he tells me that he flew in yesterday from California to help with the relief effort. He smiles when I ask what type of work he has been doing.

"Guess," he says.

"You look like the counselor type," I say.

"Not even close," he says.

"Are you an FBI agent?" I ask.

"Nope," he says. "I'll tell you because you'll never guess."

His company, he explains, manufactures a device that locates human heartbeats. The human heart emits a particular type of electrical impulse, and this machine (in ways that I am unable to understand despite his clear and patient explanation) is attuned to such a frequency. In this way, the machine enables the search-and-rescue teams to locate more effectively survivors who may be trapped underneath the rubble. "Here," he says, "I'll show you."

From his backpack he pulls out what looks like a small black, plastic radio with a silver antenna. He aims the antenna at my chest and flicks a switch.

"Now step to the left," he says. I do it.

Amazingly, the antenna slowly follows me. I move to the right, and again it traces my path. It's an incredible tool and I am moved to realize that it's not only the physical resources that are being brought to bear on the recovery effort, but intellectual and scientific ones as well.

After a quick lunch on the Spirit boat, Andrew and I split up once again. Almost immediately I run into two men standing by the New York Police Department

Memorial on the esplanade: one an electrician, the other a carpenter. Both are big, barrel-chested men; both are animated and talkative. Initially it is surprising to meet men like this: they are the first rescue workers I've met here who I could describe as "cheerful." But they are friendly and generous volunteers, so their cheerfulness is welcome, not offensive.

They begin by telling me stories of their work. The electrician works with his crew in one of the many office buildings surrounding the site that are preparing to welcome businesses back in a few weeks. And, indeed, miles of thick, black, electrical cable now snake across the esplanade, covered by rough plywood boards that enable the little green jeeps and larger vehicles to pass over them more smoothly. Abruptly, he stops talking about his work and asks if I knew that a number of people were trapped in the tower elevators after the two planes hit. He and the carpenter, suddenly speaking softly, surmise—based on their expertise—what must have happened to them.

They speak of the many people who jumped from the buildings, and say that it was good that the media did not show this, though such footage is being shown overseas. The families of the victims have had a hard enough time, and what point would there be? says the carpenter. His electrician friend nods silently, his eyes fixed on the pavement.

Animated once more, the carpenter tells me that he had watched the collapse of the first tower from his apartment in Brooklyn and raced here on foot to help, even as the second tower was collapsing. Many construction workers, he says, died here. Think, he says, of how many laborers and craftsmen were working in the building at the time: carpenters, plumbers, welders, construction workers, electricians. "It wasn't just office workers," he says. "It was our guys, too."

After an hour, I meet up with Andrew and together we start on our way home. Along the way, we pass two young firemen.

"How are you guys doing?" I ask them.

"No," says one of them, who places a friendly hand on my shoulder. "How are *you* doin', Father?"

I am silent, for the question catches me off guard.

"You guys are probably not used to seeing this kind of thing," he says. "How are you feeling, Father?"

I am taken aback as much by the question as by the one who asks.

How am I feeling? How am I doing? Whatever I'm feeling, the fireman who stands before me is feeling it a thousand times more. However I'm doing, I'm not expected to work in a place where my friends lie dead in a pile of rubble. However I'm doing, I'm not working in a job where I am expected to recover corpses and to retrieve body remains. And whatever I'm feeling, I'm getting a good night's sleep and am not expected to work, essentially, around the clock.

What I'm feeling is a deep sense of admiration for the man who stands in front of me.

So I say, I'm fine. It's you rescue workers who are doing the tough work.

"Everyone does what they can," he says. "Just make sure you take care of yourself, Father."

And I think, here is what it means to be an adult Christian: to live life with an equal mixture of bravery and pity.

SUNDAY, SEPTEMBER 23

This morning I am here with Joe and Chris, two young Jesuits from Fordham University. Part of Jesuit training includes philosophy studies, and there is a large community of Jesuit seminarians studying at Fordham, for whom working at Ground Zero has become a kind of temporary ministry. Their companionship has been a signal blessing for me, and I have been moved by the generous response of their community. It is also good to work here alongside other Jesuits: it's the kind of ministry that Jesuits have long done—in places of crisis, in areas where the institutional Church is just beginning to organize, in regions of great need. For Joe, this is his second time at Ground Zero; for Chris, his first.

While the three of us talk to a National Guardsman from upstate New York, a giant tractor-trailer heaves to a stop on the street beside us. A steelworker with a few days' growth of beard climbs down from his rig and approaches Joe. "Can I speak with you, Father?" As

Chris and I move away to offer them a measure of privacy, the man embraces Joe and begins to weep.

As the two of them talk, I notice that we are standing beside an office building whose first-floor windows are covered with dozens of messages. Still thickly coated with soot, the dirty windows around the site have become a place for the rescue workers to express a variety of emotions. "God Bless America" says one in tall, loopy letters. "Rescue 1 Heroes," "We Will Never Forget," "Down But Not Out," and "Payback's a Bitch, Osama."

After ten minutes Joe rejoins us. The man, he says quietly, is here for the first time. All I did today, he tells Joe, was drive my truck into the site, and people were cheering for me. I don't deserve that, he says. I'm just a regular guy. I'm no hero.

Joe, visibly moved, wonders if he said the right things or counseled the man the right way. Chris and I tell Joe that he did a good job by listening so intently to the man, who felt comfortable enough with Joe to weep. In places like this, I say, God seems to know which people need to be brought together. I remember the African American man who sought out Pawel last week after our Mass.

"Grace is everywhere," I say. "Especially here." And I am convinced of this. We walk only a few steps before catching sight of a white trailer. On its side are three large black-and-yellow placards bearing the name of the company that owns the van: "Grace Industries."

"Grace really *is* everywhere," says Joe, smiling.

As we approach the rubble pile, we pass a small stand of trees, now partitioned from the site by a six-foot chain-link fence. Hidden behind the Grace Industries van, the trees would easily escape our notice if we weren't looking for them. But I had spotted them a few days before, and want Chris and Joe to see them as well.

The little trees, each only six or seven feet high, have been flattened by the tremendous force of the collapse of the Trade Center buildings and now lie lifeless on the ground. Tangled into their spindly branches are hundreds of sheets of paper—office memos, copies of e-mails, résumés, financial reports, personal letters, expense accounts. When I had first stumbled upon these trees, the papers were dry and wrinkled, like dirty leaves. Now, after a few days during which an intermittent drizzle has fallen on the city, they appear as *papier-mâché* coating the gray branches.

Chris and Joe look on silently. "It's so sad," Chris says. "So ordinary. They didn't even suspect what was going to happen as they started their day."

• • •

The morgue is still the place where it seems that the rescue workers are most willing to talk. And today there is an even more obvious feeling of sadness and exhaustion. It seems as if people are much more willing to cry and to express emotion. Is it because it's Sunday?

We come upon two people resting on leather office chairs next to a police car outside the morgue: a slight, blond-haired woman from one of the city's Emergency Medical Service teams and a fireman who has been pulling out bodies over the last few days. The fireman says that the search for those still alive in the wreckage is rapidly drawing to a close; now it is more of a "recovery" effort. But even while admitting this, he is resolute about his job. "We need to find those remains," he says. "It really helps the families."

As he speaks, a policewoman approaches us. She is a young, Hispanic American woman, with short dark hair. "Can I ask you something?" she says to me. Of course, I say.

"Do you think that jumping from a building is suicide?"

I hesitate, struggling to think of some spiritual insight that would help her. No, it's not, I think, but how to explain this?

"No," Chris says. "They weren't trying to die, they were trying to live. They wanted to live. That's not suicide."

It's a beautiful response, and I am proud of Chris for his insight and compassion. Once again, it seems that God knows how to bring people together. The policewoman begins to weep and the E.M.S. volunteer wraps her arms tightly around her. I ask if there is someone she is thinking of and she says yes. She quietly utters her friend's name. The six of us stand in a circle and pray for her friend.

On the way to lunch on the Spirit boat, a fireman calls out to us. "Hey, Father!" A tall, red-haired man, perhaps twenty-five years old, he wears his fire company's blue T-shirt and heavy black overalls held up by suspenders. We wander over to him and introduce ourselves. He appears agitated.

"Listen," he says. "What's with all the fucking Scientologists?"

I think I know what he's talking about. On my second day here I was surprised to meet fifteen or so young men and women, some of whom looked no older than teenagers, wandering around the esplanade in bright yellow T-shirts that read: "Volunteer Minister." I had occasion to speak with one of them, a friendly young man, and noticed that another part of his T-shirt read: "Church of Scientology."

My first reaction was to wonder how they gained access, since security was, even in the first few days, tight. My second reaction was to wonder why in this place, where the overwhelming majority of firefighters are Catholic, there seemed to be ten times as many Scientologists as there were Catholic and Protestant chaplains. Later I heard from a Salvation Army volunteer that some of the rescue workers were angry because the Scientologists were—in the words of the St. Joseph chaplain— "proselytizing," that is, distributing literature to the rescue workers.

"Yeah," I say to the firefighter, "I guess I know what you mean." I tell him that I've heard from a fire chaplain that the Scientologists have been advised (by whomever tells people these things) that they were allowed to continue ministering here, but only if they stopped proselytizing.

"Good!" says the firefighter.

He continues. "I mean, I'm a fucking Catholic. I go to Mass every fucking Sunday, and it's ridiculous that there are more of those guys than priests. I mean, I wanted to see some priests! It's good to see you guys here!"

Normally, I've found that when people use that kind of language when I'm wearing a Roman collar, it's followed by an immediate (unnecessary, but appreciated) apology along the lines of "Sorry, Father." But this man seems comfortable speaking with us in this way, and the three of us are not bothered by the language. If anything, it shows that he's comfortable with us, and I am touched by his honesty and openness, especially in this setting. Far from being offended, I accept it as a compliment of sorts.

When we ask after his work, he tells us that he is stationed aboard one of the fireboats docked nearby. "Stop by and see me," he says. He adds in a whisper, "Just don't bring any of those fucking Scientologists!"

After lunch, we make our way over to the place that still feels like an open wound: the rubble pile. There is a tall, forty-ish police chief with thinning hair staring at the remaining outer walls of the towers, which today are wreathed in milky white smoke.

"Father!" he says, waving me over. He's worried about something, he says.

Yesterday, he explains, he spoke with a police chaplain who confided how depressed he was by the events of the past two weeks. The chaplain told him that because he hadn't been able to minister to anyone who had been pulled from the wreckage alive, that he wasn't doing enough.

"I told him that he was doing the best he could," says the police officer, "and that just being here was enough."

The policeman pauses. "Was that the right thing to say?"

I assure him that it was an excellent response—the perfect response in fact—and marvel at a policeman providing counseling and comfort for a priest, and at a policeman who himself wonders if he's doing enough.

• • •

Around 4:00, Joe, Chris, and I exit via the West Side Highway. As we remove our respirators and hard hats and talk about the day, Chris mentions that some of the steelworkers told him about finding a dove in the wreckage today. "They were really excited about it," he says. Chris says that while workers were excavating a small open space that had been spared in the collapse, a white dove fluttered around and flew up and away from the rubble. The men saw it as a sign, especially coming on a Sunday.

Unlike last week, there is only a small crowd cheering the police cars, fire trucks, and tractor-trailers that emerge from the site. Likewise, the number of television news vans and reporters has declined dramatically. I am sad to see this: there is still a need for the rescue workers to feel support and for the news to be disseminated. Joe says he hopes the workers are not turning into last week's story.

A mile or so from the site, we pass a chain-link fence onto which are tied hundreds of yellow ribbons, in remembrance of the victims. Dozens of "Missing Person" flyers—Xeroxed sheets with photographs and descriptions of those lost—adorn the same fence a few feet away.

As we head farther north, a man sprints toward us and climbs over the concrete divider that separates the street from the path on which we walk. He asks for a few minutes of my time. Joe and Chris move away and sit down on the curb nearby.

He is a big man, whose gray hair is pulled back into a lank ponytail. He wears dusty jeans, a dirty T-shirt, and a tan windbreaker. A steelworker with puffy, tired eyes, he has been working at the site since September 12.

Over the last few days, I've come to realize that many of the remains are found not only by firefighters and police officers but also by the steelworkers, iron-workers, and construction crews who have volunteered here. As they use their tools to slice through the huge steel I-beams littering the site, they inevitably come upon a body or body parts. But these are men whose trade has not prepared them at all for such labor, and I feel a great deal of pity for them.

The man before me tells me of the things he's seen in the rubble. "But now when I go home, I can't bear to see my wife and child," he says, with tears tracing lines down his dusty face. "Because every time I see their faces, I see the faces of the people I pull out."

It is a stunning statement that seems to encapsulate all of the emotions that people are facing here: grief, horror, confusion, pity, shock, despair. We talk more about what he has seen, and I tell him that what he's feeling is certainly natural under the hellish circumstances. And has he found any of the grief counselors down at the site?

When he shakes his head, I tell him that there are many counselors who would be able to talk with him at the site. "You can ask the fire department or police department or the Red Cross or the Salvation Army." I know that in a short conversation I cannot do much: I am not a trained mental-health professional, psychologist, or psychiatrist.

I desperately want this poor man to get some help, so I ask him again if he will promise to seek out one of the grief counselors. He nods his head vigorously. We talk some more and he wipes away his tears. He stands up and shakes my hand deliberately.

"You know," he says, "I used to be Catholic. But now I sort of mix it with Indian religions. You know, Native American stuff." Suddenly his ponytail takes on a different look. "Because I figure it's all one God in the end. You know?"

WEDNESDAY, SEPTEMBER 26

Today I have come with two other young Jesuits from Fordham—Brian has been a Jesuit for only two years; Joe, for three. This will be the first visit to the site for both of them. They meet me at my Jesuit community in midtown Manhattan and, as has become our habit, we pray for the work of the day. When we approach the first checkpoint, we say a prayer to ask the intercession of Pedro Arrupe, and we pass easily.

While the memory of death is never far from anyone's mind here, the area surrounding the ruined World Trade Center is beginning to look more like a construction site and less like the chaotic disaster scene of the first week. Many fire companies have pulled firefighters back to their station houses (as there are always fires in the city to be combated), and many firefighters now admit that their "buddies" will probably not be rescued alive from the collapsed towers. There are also fewer police officers, Army personnel, and National Guards-men on duty. At the same time, the site is even more crowded with heavy machinery: towering super-cranes, rumbling backhoes, noisy front-end loaders, mammoth excavators, colossal flatbed trailers.

And there is a surfeit of specialized, technical teams now on the job, new faces, and new skills: engineers and surveyors inspecting the buildings, health inspectors ana-lyzing the soil and air, electricians attempting to mend failed wiring, and telephone workers laying thick cables across the wet roads surrounding the Trade Center.

We meet, as we have in the past, men and women who appear calm and relaxed on the surface, but who underneath suffer intensely and uniquely. One fireman, standing by the morgue, chats amiably about his family, his work, and finally, his friends in his company. I ask him if he lost anyone in the disaster.

"My best friend," he says quietly. "I've known him all my life."

It's breathtaking to hear such words uttered only a few feet from where his friend was killed. I ask his friend's name and we pray aloud for him.

Just then, a fire department official in a windbreaker runs up to me, breathless.

"Father," he says, "we've just found a last-rites kit. We don't know what to do with it. Do you think it might be Father Mike's kit?"

Father Mychal Judge, a Franciscan priest, was a longtime and much loved chaplain for the New York City Fire Department. After hearing news of the terrorist attacks, Father Judge rushed to the scene, knowing that there would be many in need of his services. Shortly after offering the last rites to a fireman killed by a person who had leapt from Tower One, Father Judge suffered a fatal heart attack. The firemen carried his body from the wreckage directly to St. Peter's Church, where he was laid on the altar, his fireman's hat resting on his chest: a visible symbol of sacrifice and self-emptying. When the names of casualties were announced, Father Judge was listed first: 00001. One fireman told me that he thought Father Mike needed to arrive in heaven first—to welcome in the rest of his buddies later.

A photographer happened to be on the scene at the time and snapped a photo of rescue workers carrying out Father Judge on a cheap plastic chair. It is a stunning photo: a *Pietà* of sorts. Supported by five big men covered in ash, Father Judge sits slumped on the chair, his head bowed, as if his long and arduous job has been completed. On the right of the photo is an official from the Office of Emergency Management, one of the many governmental agencies overseeing the rescue efforts. But the fold of the man's jacket slightly obscures the agency's logo, and I am amazed to see that rather than "OEM," it appears instead to read "OFM," that is, the traditional abbreviation for "Orders of Franciscans Minor," Father Judge's religious order.

When I suggest that the firefighter bring Father Judge's last-rites kit to one of the fire chaplains for safe-keeping, he sprints back toward the pile.

Nearby is a police officer who has been working at the morgue. He sits heavily on a discarded office chair whose torn fabric is still covered with ash. "You know what they pulled out today?" he asks me. "Animal bones."

I'm not sure what he means, so I ask.

"Well," he explains, "they spent a long time trying to figure out what they had found. Then it hit them: they were bones from a pig."

I stare at him, not understanding.

"It was spare ribs," he says. "Probably from Windows on the World."

Somehow this shocks me anew. I hadn't thought at all of the people in Windows on the World, the popular restaurant perched on the uppermost floors of Tower One. The realization that at the moment the plane struck, a cook might have been busy preparing the day's food, in his clean white smock and black-and-white checked pants, chatting with his fellow workers in the restaurant's warm kitchen, fills me with great sadness. Like the stray papers we have seen littering the plaza, the abrupt ending of these ordinary activities seems suffused with special pathos.

Today, for the first time, I walk into the area that lies directly east of the Trade Center, which has seen less of an organized cleanup effort. As a result, we view the scene much as it must have been on September 11. Joe, Brian, and I walk through the small, quiet side streets: here the windows of the neighborhood pubs are still covered with grime and the heavy cloth awnings hanging over restaurant windows are savagely torn or have simply collapsed. Wrapped around a lamppost is a horribly twisted set of Venetian blinds. It reminds us of the terrific violence of the initial blasts, even blocks away, in this area "protected" by interposed buildings.

A parking garage fronting the street offers up cars caked with dried ash; paper clogs the chain-link fence that surrounds the garage. It's hard not to wonder if the cars remain here because their owners have not been allowed access or because their owners were lost in the terrorist attacks. I recall a friend telling me that at commuter rail stations throughout Connecticut and New Jersey, some commuters have begun writing on the dirty windshields of abandoned cars the number of days that the cars have remained in the lot, awaiting their owners.

Back near the rubble pile we meet two chaplains working for the FBI One is from their office in Houston, one from Alabama. They tell us how even the FBI agents are finding it difficult to be here. "Worse than Oklahoma City," says one. "Yeah," says the other, who opens his mouth to say something, and then just shakes his head.

The Alabama chaplain reaches into his pocket and pulls out a small lapel pin. "This is so you remember that the people in Alabama are thinking about you." It is a blue pin shaped like the state with a yellow seat belt painted across. "Buckle up," it says.

As he hands me this, a group of roughly fifty people pass in front of us. They are accompanied by just as many escorts, men and women wearing navy blue windbreakers with lettering saying "NYPD" or "FDNY." I wonder who they are. Residents of the area returning to their apartments? Most walk in pairs, wearing too-large windbreakers and ill-fitting hard hats. New volunteers? Most walk with downcast faces. Then I see that most are weeping. I realize, with a start, that these are the family members of the victims of the attack, visiting the site for the first time. I had read just this morning that many were now being brought to the site.

The two FBI chaplains fall silent and remove their hard hats. I do likewise. We stand quietly as the family members slowly walk by us, on their way to the graves of their fathers, their mothers, their brothers, their sisters, their sons, their daughters, their husbands, their wives, their friends. On their way to look upon a sight that will burn itself into their memories and remain with them for the rest of their lives.

FRIDAY, SEPTEMBER 28

As I enter the site this afternoon with Joe and Anthony, two Jesuit seminarians, I notice that, once again, things have changed noticeably. As soon as we pass the perimeter, Joe, who has been here twice before, comments that we are seeing far fewer rescue workers.

Those still at the site, however, continue to work long hours. One policeman mentions that his precinct is now sending down nine or ten officers each day, with each officer working twelve-hour shifts. But, as almost everyone points out, that figure doesn't include the hour of commuting both ways. So fourteen-hour days are common. Still, he says, he doesn't mind coming down.

"Everyone is so friendly," he says, almost apologetically. "I like being here." He pauses. "It's better than being back in the South Bronx. They don't appreciate us as much."

I am surprised; I had thought that the public's perception of the NYPD and FDNY had altered dramatically since September 11: I had heard stories of the police being cheered in neighborhoods where they had formerly been held in contempt.

"Yeah," says the officer, "that lasted about a week."

Physically, the site has changed dramatically; indeed, the rate of change accelerates with every visit. The hundreds of chairs used by rescue workers that had filled the esplanade have vanished. Ten-foot-high stacks of plywood boards, to be used for boarding up the hundreds of shattered windows, now cover a large area behind the World Financial Center. Heavy concrete barriers line the docks at the marina. The chapel is cleared of any remaining boxes of supplies, the dusty chairs are back inside, and its door is now tightly locked. Sanitation trucks roam the site, sweeping and spraying the streets as they go; as a result, the area is now surprisingly clean and largely free of the clouds of ash that had blown about the site during the first weeks.

As the area has become less obstructed by debris, cleaner, and perhaps safer, the city is also bringing in more groups of family members who wish to visit Ground Zero. A sanitation worker tells us that a new group arrives roughly every three hours.

Although we have witnessed this before, it is wrenching to watch. The families are first ferried to the docks on police department boats. They come in groups of fifty or sixty at a time, escorted by firefighters, police officers, and professional counselors. Many of the older men and women walk arm in arm, it appears, with a son or daughter.

They pass behind the World Financial Center, behind the collapsed Winter Garden atrium, and finally to the remains of the towers, where workers still labor. After spending time at the site, they slowly retrace their steps; but on their return, they pause at a set of concrete steps that have been turned into a makeshift shrine near the Police Memorial. There they lay blue and pink teddy bears that often bear messages written on them with magic marker: "Good-bye." "I love you." "We miss you." "Good-bye, Daddy." Piles of freshly cut flowers wrapped in crinkly cellophane are laid at the foot of the chain-link fence. After standing before the memorial for a brief while, the groups return to the boats and are ferried away.

Activity ceases and the site falls silent whenever such groups pass. The police clear a path for them, and the rescue workers pause at their tasks: truck drivers stop their rigs, electricians set down their cable, the sanitation workers halt their sweeping, the carpenters lay down their hammers. All of the firefighters and police officers remove their hats as they pass by.

Everyone, like me, seems overwhelmed with pathos for them. And today I think of my own father, who died of lung cancer only two months ago. He had been sick for many months before his death in late July.

How can I explain the intense sadness that I felt standing beside my father's hospital bed and watching him die? To see him suffer and weep. To watch him struggle for breath. To see his embarrassment at being incontinent, having to be fed, having to be dressed. Yet, in the midst of my father's arduous journey toward death, there came moments of unexpected grace: in the form of reconciliation and forgiveness and love. Dying seemed to make my father more tender, more open, and more human. And his nine months of illness drew my family together in surprising ways and, also, allowed me to see both my father and mother in a new and clearer light. In the end, I think, he was prepared to die, and my mother and sister and I were prepared to say good-bye. His death, after such a long illness, was almost a relief; his funeral for me was both healing and consoling.

How far from these mourners is that experience of loss. For many, there was no chance to say good-bye, to

kiss a father on the head before he leaves this world,
squeeze a wife's familiar hand, stroke a daughter's hair,
give a son a drink of cold water, a lover a hug. Piled on
to this sorrow is the shock of seeing the site: the place of
their violent death. It is so far from my experience that,
as they walk slowly by us, all I can do is pray.

After a group of forty or so makes its way past, the
three of us continue toward the site, stopping to talk with
rescue workers. Joe mentions that when we were last
here, he was able to move in closer to the rubble pile than
I had thought possible. He suggests returning today to
investigate if there might be some new possibilities for
ministry. We ask a group of very young soldiers in helmets and camouflage if we might be able to move past
the cordon and up to the rubble pile, and they nod.

As we draw closer, we maneuver our way past the
tractor-trailers and flatbed trucks parked directly next to
the site, awaiting the next load of crumpled steel girders.
We speak—shout, really—to three truck drivers over the
deafening noise of machinery: cranes, forklifts, front-end
loaders, backhoes, saws, drills, welding tools. The men
wear respirators, as a noxious smell still pervades this
area closest to the ruined towers: newspapers have been
reporting with increasing regularity on the hazardous
fumes that one might inhale here. We press our masks

tightly against our faces, and I smell the cheap plastic of the pink respirator.

Only a few feet from the pile, we look around, and I feel the same stab of fear that I felt on the first day. The skeletal remains of the tower walls jut angrily into the open sky, so high that it seems a wonder they do not topple. Surrounding them are two piles (nine stories? ten?) of rubble: tons of glass, steel, metal, and the sad detritus of thousands of offices—crushed computers, torn carpets, splintered doors, smashed desks, mangled file cabinets, broken chairs. Towering cranes carry away girders as firemen spray streams of water on the still-smoldering, stinking rubble. We speak with the men only briefly, as they tell us it is too dangerous for us to be here. Before leaving, we pray together, in shouts.

Afterwards we split up—Joe and Anthony together, me on my own. Among other people that afternoon, I meet three New York City sanitation workers, all wearing bright green uniforms. They tell me how much work they did in the first few days after September 11, clearing the site of the debris that rained down following the attack. "It was hard to be here," one says. "We saw all sorts of things." I think he is speaking about seeing bodies and body parts, but it seems as if that's all he wants to say about the matter, so I just nod.

All three seem justly proud of their contribution here, and I feel a sudden surge of affection for them. One of the sanitation workers wears a gold cross on a chain around his neck. "Hey Father," he says suddenly, "let me ask you something. Why do you think God let this happen?"

I've heard this question many times over the last few weeks, both at the site and away from it. It is what theologians call "the question of evil." In its simplest form the question is: If God is good, then why is there evil and suffering? Others have framed the problem in this way: If God is all-good, then he cannot be all-powerful, because he obviously cannot prevent evil. Or, if God is all-powerful, then he is not all-good, since he can prevent evil but chooses not to do so. And though saints, theologians, and philosophers have struggled with this question for centuries, there is no satisfactory answer. Nevertheless, for the believer it is a question that must be confronted. Or, more aptly, it is a mystery that must be pondered.

For Christians, one response to the question comes in meditating on the story of Jesus of Nazareth—for there is much in the story of Jesus to console those who suffer.

First, one encounters a loving God who so desired to be with us, who so desired to reveal himself to us, that he became one of us. But by taking on our humanity, he also opened himself to suffering.

And so God, one could say, knows what it is like to suffer. Jesus of Nazareth, in the prophetic words of Isaiah, was a "man acquainted with grief." Many Christians find consolation in this notion of a God who has experienced and understands our pain. Like a close friend who has been through an illness or tragedy that we now face, we feel comforted by this shared experience and can allow that friend to share in our suffering more easily.

One can also say that for Christians, Jesus of Nazareth provides us with a model of how to live a life that will inevitably include suffering. In his life on earth, Jesus grasped that suffering is part of the human experience. And his own suffering was borne not only with patience but also with the hope that comes from an intimate relationship with God. Moreover, when confronted with the suffering of others, Jesus' first—and instinctive—response was to heal and to console. In Jesus, we are provided a model of compassion, a word that, of course, means "to suffer with."

But most of all, the story of Jesus includes the mystery of the Resurrection, which shows us that suffering and death do not have the final say. The power of God and of life is always stronger than death or evil: this is the message of the Resurrection and, ultimately, of Christianity. Love is stronger than hate. Good is stronger than evil. And life is stronger than death. The Resurrection is the ultimate symbol of hope in a world that admits the existence of suffering.

But in the face of suffering, I have found, especially here, that it is better to allow people to come to their own understanding of the meaning of suffering. Offering quick answers or glib theological responses— compassionate though they may be—may not be the best thing for people to hear as they struggle through the early stages of loss or grief. Far better to give them the freedom to ponder this mystery first in their own hearts. You cannot impose meaning on someone's suffering; you can only accompany them as they find meaning.

So before I respond to the sanitation worker, I ask him how he makes sense of his experience. Where does he find God in all of this?

The question seems to catch him off guard, and he pauses for a few seconds.

"I think," he says finally, "that God wants us to see the good here. Because everyone's really pulling together. I hope we don't forget this." His friends nod.

I agree with him. And I tell him and his friends that I don't believe that God wills evil or suffering, but that in times of suffering we are somehow more open to seeing God. Maybe it's because we feel more vulnerable, with our normal defenses down and our egos stripped bare, that we are able to see God more readily. While experiencing God in a new way is not why evil happens, during such moments we can see God in new ways, if we are open to doing so. Experiencing God, in other words, is not the *why* of suffering but the *what* of suffering. I think of my father, facing an illness and desperately wishing to be healed, but nevertheless finding himself touched by God in ways that he seemed unable to experience when he was healthy. I think of the breaking of bread on the Spirit boat. I think of the generosity of the rescue workers. I think of the fireman who seeks out Mass. I think of the sign of the "Body of Christ." I think of the people drawn together here. I think of Flick, of the fireman from Florida, and of the cheering people at the barricades: all signs of God's presence in the world.

"It's the good and the bad, both of them, right here," says his friend, the sanitation worker, who points to the remains of the twin towers.

I can't help thinking: If any people still doubt the reality of evil in the world, let them come to the World Trade Center.

And if any still doubt the presence of God in the world, let them come to the World Trade Center.

Sunday, October 7

This morning I celebrate Mass at the local Jesuit parish, St. Ignatius Loyola. The first reading is breathtaking; when I had first read it in preparation for my homily, it was as if I had never seen it before. It's taken from the Book of Habakkuk:

> Why do you let me see ruin; why must
> I look on misery? Destruction and vio-
> lence are before me; there is strife and
> clamorous discord.

During the homily I speak about the terrorist attacks, saying that even in Habakkuk's time believers asked questions about suffering, about violence, about death. It is an integral part of being a believer. And so the question, "Where is God?" is also a natural one. In response, I speak a bit about my own experience of finding God at the site and of witnessing the presence of the Holy Spirit.

Though I know that some in the congregation have lost friends and family in the attack, and do not wish to minimize this devastating loss, I also feel it's important to speak about where God seems to be revealing himself.

Afterwards a man approaches me and says quietly that he and his wife both worked in Tower One—he on the fortieth floor and she on the fiftieth. My heart sinks; I don't see his wife anywhere in the congregation. But he registers my alarm and quickly adds that she is fine; they made it out together. So here he is this morning, looking healthy, standing with his hand placed tenderly on his young son's shoulder. But it's an unsettling moment, for while I think of God's care for him and his wife, I also think of the arbitrariness of who escaped and who didn't.

After Mass I make my way down to the site, along with Tom, a Jesuit priest. On the subway ride, I mention to Tom that last week was the first opportunity I've had to spend time with a few friends I had not seen since September 11. Before last week, I was either working at the site, preparing to return, or catching up on the work that had piled up during my time away from my desk. And I was moved by the ways in which each one of my friends was affected by the attacks.

At an Ethiopian restaurant on the West Side, for example, I meet up with Jim, a college friend who is now a human rights lawyer. Over dinner, along with two of Jim's friends, the conversation turns inevitably to the events of the past few weeks. I'm particularly interested in Jim's perspective, as he has worked around the globe in countries torn by violence and terrorism—Cambodia, Sri Lanka, Burma, Bosnia. Like everyone, Jim says he's felt the sense of tension and confusion that now pervades the city. And he suggests that for the first time Americans are confronted with a situation that, sadly, exists for many in the world all the time.

One of Jim's friends mentions that she had carried over meatloaf sandwiches to the fire station in her neighborhood. But, she said sadly, she feels as if she could do more. I tell her what I've been telling so many friends: that any effort is valuable and meaningful. And, again, that everyone seems to feel that they can't do enough— even the rescue workers at the site. But I am surprised when her eyes fill with tears; I realize I have touched upon a deep reservoir of emotion.

Another friend, Lisa, is a journalist working on a magazine story about the employees in Windows on the World. It is, I think, a fine way of approaching the tragedy of September 11, allowing readers to grasp the stunning cross section of people who were killed in the attacks: chefs, cooks, and busboys, as well as business persons, tourists, and other guests breakfasting at the restaurant. Lisa tells me that she is extremely tense after the attacks and, what's more, finds herself overwhelmed by the emotions of those whom she interviews. She speaks, for example, to an elderly woman whose son and daughter provided and cared for her. Both worked in Windows on the World. What will she do now? My journalist friend now finds herself counseling this indigent mother, who has no one left to talk to.

Most arrestingly, I speak with a close friend named Roger, who works as a musician at St. Ignatius. On September 11, he was on his way to a school for blind children, where his son is a student, near Sixth Avenue and 11th Street, in Greenwich Village. Immediately I conjure up a mental image of the area, and realize that the intersection Roger describes offers an unparalleled and unobstructed view of the towers. I grimace when I think of the view, and I ask him what it was like on that morning.

At first, Roger says that he hears the "tearing" sound of a low-flying jet and thinks to himself how out of place this sound is in Lower Manhattan. Someone standing next to him on the street curses mildly and makes a comment about "that stupid pilot." Roger thinks: If the plane continues on that flight path, there's a good chance that it might hit something. Others on the street, alerted by the unusually loud noise of the huge airplane, watch silently along with Roger, "for a good five seconds," before the shocking impact. "It was very quiet then," he says. Instantly he runs back to the school to collect his son. He tells a teacher that a plane has hit the World Trade Center, finding it hard to believe even as he is reporting this to her.

When Roger emerges with his son, traffic has now halted in the middle of Sixth Avenue. People emerge from their cars and stare at the burning tower. "This is real," he thinks. He stands watching, beside his son, for twenty minutes, wondering what to do. At the approach of the other plane, people suddenly cry out, weep, and kneel on the sidewalk with their hands pressed tightly over their ears. "When the screaming started, it was as if people were finally acknowledging what they were seeing." Roger sees the second plane slam into the tower and—he remembers—feels the urge to vomit. He stands with his blind son, who hears but does not see what has happened.

He quickly decides to walk the forty blocks uptown to his apartment, knowing already that the subways would be shut down. His son asks to stop for a soda in a drugstore, and there Roger hears news of the attack on the Pentagon. Upon arriving at his apartment building, he is told that both buildings have collapsed, and he is overwhelmed by a feeling of terror. From his terrace he watches the inky plume of smoke grow to monstrous size over Lower Manhattan, and thinks over and over of two friends who work in the towers, who he is sure are dead. (He will discover days later that they are fine; one is the husband I speak with at Mass this morning.)

We say good-bye standing on the street outside the little restaurant where we've just eaten. A plane passes overhead and we both look toward the sky, scanning it briefly but nervously. We look at each other, in surprise. "I never used to notice planes before," says Roger.

• • •

Now, this morning, as I walk around the site with Tom, something becomes clear to me, something that I've thought about during the last few visits here: the type of ministry we have been doing here seems less urgent, less needed. The groups with whom my brother Jesuits and I have been ministering—the large numbers of rescue workers who were catching their breaths after long hours of work, who were resting outside the morgue, who were on their way to the Spirit boat for a bite to eat—have diminished dramatically. The firefighters have almost all returned to their firehouses, the police back to their precincts. It's a different place: even the Spirit boat has gone.

To be sure, there is still a great deal of activity around the site, as even larger and taller cranes have been brought in to remove the rubble and accomplish the recovery work.

But the operation is tighter, and seems more focused. Today Tom and I meet what one could call the "next shift": engineers, security personnel, architects, surveyors, and construction workers, many of whom are concentrating on preparing the surrounding buildings for their re-opening.

Moreover, the effort to provide counseling to the remaining rescue workers is now highly coordinated, its structures and procedures more firmly in place. As it turns out, a Jesuit friend is helping to run one of the family counseling offices of the Red Cross, and tells me of the wonderfully organized work they are doing here.

In short, I feel that we are less needed. At times, it almost seems as if Tom and I are in the way. So today, something that I have been suspecting seems to be confirmed: that God is asking us to step aside and let others continue the work at the site.

So we spend only a few hours here this afternoon. We walk behind the World Financial Center and see that St. Joseph's Chapel is cleaned, its chairs in place, and preparing to re-open. Vast piles of plywood boards still sit behind the Winter Garden, but most of the damaged windows have been successfully boarded up. As teams of electricians work on the surrounding office towers, employees of Merrill Lynch and American Express, wearing neatly pressed pants and clean Oxford-cloth shirts, wander in and out of the buildings.

We make our way over to the area near the NYPD memorial. The steps across from the memorial have now become a sprawling shrine to the victims, and the teddy bears, flowers, photographs, and notes left by the families and friends fill the area. Tom approaches the area and kneels to pray.

I am surprised to run into a police officer whom I had met a few weeks ago. She asks if I remember her. I do; she is the one who had asked the painful questions about suicide. "What your friend said to me really helped," she says, and shakes my hand. I am happy to hear this, and promise her that I will tell Chris, the Jesuit who was with me that day.

Finally, it seems like it's time to leave. Now, almost one month after the tragedy, there are regulations in place for leaving the site. One needs to have one's boots scrubbed and rinsed by hazardous-materials (or "hazmat") teams that are stationed near the exits. Automobiles and trucks are sprayed with high-powered hoses to remove toxic materials that they might inadvertently carry away. By contrast, I remember leaving the site during the first few days: traipsing into the subway station covered with dust and simply throwing my clothes in the washing machine at home. Like many of the relief workers, I have also started to wonder, and worry, about what my friends and I may have ingested or inhaled or touched.

On the way out, as we walk up West Street, I am surprised to see something that I have not seen before. One of the flatbed trucks leaving the site carries mangled steel I-beams. This is common enough. But as it passes I am stunned to see that the huge girders are still steaming. A fine line of white smoke rises from the still-hot metal.

That image says to me, *Look*. Look at this new thing that you haven't seen. Look at how little you really have seen and experienced in this place. Look at how little you have really understood. Look, and do not try to say how much you've seen. Do not try to say how much you understand. Because you have seen little. And you understand little.

My experience at the World Trade Center was narrow, limited, and circumscribed. I was not there on September 11. I did not watch the airplanes slam into the side of the buildings. I did not have to run down flights and flights of stairs, fearing for my life. I did not see people jumping from buildings. I did not see the towers fall. I did not lose any friends or family or co-workers in the collapse of the buildings. I was not overcome by the choking wall of dust and smoke that raced through the plaza. I did not have to remove body parts and remains in the hours after the tragedy. I was not a doctor or nurse or paramedic tending to the injured. I was not a firefighter or rescue worker pulling out victims or my buddies from the rubble. I was not a U.S. Army soldier or a National Guard volunteer flown in from hundreds of miles away, expected to work long hours. I did not have to watch people die.

And I spent only a few days working at the site. I could come and go as I wanted and when I wanted. I was not an exhausted firefighter mourning the loss of my best friend. I was not a police officer on sixteen-hour shifts agonizing about suicides she had seen. I was not a worn-out steelworker who finds himself unable to look into his wife's eyes.

I have not seen much.

This is what I think as the flatbed truck rumbles past us, bearing away the steaming girders.

Of the suffering, the sadness, the horror, the evil, I have seen little.

But of the charity, the hope, the love, and the good, I have seen more than I can tell.

ACKNOWLEDGMENTS

I would like to express a deep gratitude to my brother Jesuits with whom I worked during the period described in these pages: Bob Reiser, S.J., Andrew Wawrzyn, S.J., Joe Palmisano, S.J., Phillip Ganir, S.J., Pawel Adamczyk, S.J., Chris Hadley, S.J., Joe Riordan, S.J., Brian Dunkle, S.J., Anthony Soo Hoo, S.J., and Tom Reese, S.J. Their companionship, generosity, and support marked for me another sign of God's presence. Thanks also to Monsignor Mark Giordano, who enabled us, through the kind offices of the Port Authority, to gain access to the site and continue ministering to the rescue workers.

As for the manuscript itself, many thanks to John Donohue, S.J., for his careful review and to Joseph McAuley for his patient help with the typing and editing. Thanks to Jeremy Langford, Steve Hrycyniak, and Kass Dotterweich of Sheed & Ward for their encouragement and advice. Thanks also to Louis Boccardi and Charles Zoeller of the Associated Press, and to photographer Graham Morrison for the image used on the cover.

Most of all, I would like to thank the firefighters, police officers, rescue workers, and volunteers for revealing what it means to live a life of dedication, service, and love.

ABOUT THE AUTHOR

The Rev. James Martin, S.J., is a Jesuit priest and an associate editor of *America*, the national Catholic magazine. A graduate of the Wharton School of the University of Pennsylvania, he worked for six years in corporate finance before entering the Society of Jesus in 1988. During his Jesuit training, he worked with homeless men and women in Boston, street-gang members in Chicago, and for two years with East African refugees in Nairobi, Kenya. After completing his studies at Weston Jesuit School of Theology in Cambridge, Massachusetts, he was ordained a priest in 1999. Father Martin is the author of *In Good Company: The Fast Track from the Corporate World to Poverty, Chastity, and Obedience* (Sheed & Ward, 2000), *This Our Exile: A Spiritual Journey with the Refugees of East Africa* (Orbis Books, 1999), and editor of *How Can I Find God?* (Liguori, 1997).